essentia

Help Your 5–7 Year Old Learn to Spell

Help Your 5–7 Year Old Learn to Spell

Ken Adams

PARENTS' ESSENTIALS

Published in 2000 by
How To Books Ltd, 3 Newtec Place,
Magdalen Road, Oxford OX4 1RE, United Kingdom
Tel: (01865) 793806   Fax: (01865) 248780
email: info@howtobooks.co.uk
www.howtobooks.co.uk

British Library Cataloguing in Publication Data.
A catalogue record for this book is available from
the British Library.

Edited by Julie Nelson
Cover design by Shireen Nathoo Design
Produced for How To Books by Deer Park Productions
Typeset by PDQ Typesetting, Newcastle-under-Lyme, Staffordshire
Printed and bound by Hillman Printers, Frome, Somerset

NOTE: The material contained in this book is set out in good faith
for general guidance and no liability can be accepted for loss or ex-
pense incurred as a result of relying in particular circumstances on
statements made in the book. The laws and regulations are complex
and liable to change, and readers should check the current position
with the relevant authorities before making personal arrangements.

ESSENTIALS *is an imprint of*
How To Books

Contents

Preface   **7**

1 How your child learns to spell   **9**
Working from the simple to the
   complex   9
Real-life learning   9
Grouping together similar sounds
   and letter patterns   10
Isolating concepts   11
Confused scenario   12
Step-wise learning   12
Interest and concentration   13

2 Phonic spelling   **15**
Forming three-letter phonic words   19
You can try these with your child   21
Testing for phonic letters and sounds   23

3 Learning double blends   **24**
Double blend beginnings   24
Trying your child with double blends   26
Some double blend endings   28
Try your child with these   28
Try these   29

4 Magic 'e' and more beginnings   **33**
Adding a magic 'e' to change the
   object name   33
Some more beginnings   36

5 Middles and endings   **39**

Middles   39

Endings   41

Try these   47

**6 Puzzles, games and crosswords to
teach spelling**   **51**

Crosswords   51

Word searches   57

Rhyming games   60

Preface

The trend towards helping your child at home has grown considerably over the past few years. Parents wish to encourage and help to interest their child in learning in areas like reading, spelling, basic maths and writing. They feel that if they can even out their child's concerns about what they learn at school, then they will approach schoolwork with confidence and greater enjoyment. As any concerned parent, they wish their child to fulfil their potential, particularly in areas that they consider of prime importance.

Spelling is one of these areas, and the early years of reading, writing and spelling is the area addressed by this book. It aims to help a parent to fill in the learning gaps for the child and to boost their knowledge of word structure. Parents will learn how to build a word knowledge in a step-wise manner so that learning is easy and enjoyable.

Spelling can be a difficult subject for some children. With knowledgeable guidance, a child will certainly flourish in the area of spelling. The aim of this book is to ensure that the parent knows how to achieve this. Such early learning arouses interest and raises the enjoyment level of learning. It also gives a kick start to your child's confidence for when they start school.

There is no suggestion of interfering with play and natural enjoyment, but rather of being aware of how your child's potential can be realised through already established and enjoyed activities.

Ken Adams

1 How Your Child Learns to Spell

Spelling follows reading, and in the beginning the processes are closely interwoven. Simple spelling is of the phonic variety:

c – a – t   spells cat

WORKING FROM THE SIMPLE TO THE COMPLEX

This basic form of spelling is easily picked up by most learners. After a little practice, they recognise the patterns that result from the consistent continuation of sound and shape of the letter. This is the simple area of spelling. Any reasonable reader with a good grounding in phonics is able to recognise three-letter words consisting of consonant, then phonic vowel and then consonant. In spelling terms, these words represent simple aspects and it helps to build on this base in a step-wise fashion towards the more complex. For example, **cat** can be built towards **clap** or **chat**. Later, complex words can be recognised as having these phonic elements – **catapult** or **catastrophe**. Cat can even be recognised as **within** words – **scatter**; or at the end of words – **polecat**.

REAL-LIFE LEARNING

However, there is no *particular* route to learn spelling. There are patterns to recognise – for example, 'magic e' changes the sound of a vowel in some words, or 'ai' is often said as 'ay' – but there are several possible routes to follow. At the beginning, it is best to keep things simple, to concentrate on phonic words, and to learn through simple groupings of letters within words. In particular, it is necessary to 'peg' words, as is done in reading. d – o – g is linked to the picture of a dog, so that the word links with the concrete or real-life body of knowledge in memory. Without this link, memorising of spelling patterns is made more difficult, because most of a child's learning up to this point has been through real-life experience. It is important to keep this link with real life as long as possible, so phonic sounds are best learnt through words that represent real objects. 'Man' or 'pan' is therefore more memorable than 'tan', and 'bag' is usually more memorable than 'lag' or 'nag'.

A picture drawn to accompany the learning of a spelling is inevitably helpful, and the better known an object is to your child, the easier is the word learnt. For example, 'dog' is usually better known and learnt than 'hog' or 'bog'.

GROUPING TOGETHER SIMILAR SOUNDS AND LETTER PATTERNS

After the phonic stage of spelling using so-called 'short' vowels ('a' for apple, 'e' for egg, etc.), there are long vowel and other vowel sounds to be learnt.

Car, far, are, artist, **par**ting have the similar sounding **ar** sound and form, and such a grouping makes memorising easier. However, other vowel sounds do not easily fit into a recognisable pattern, and make spelling difficult – **a**ll, P**au**l, cr**aw**l, for example.

Formal spelling lists that group in this fashion can accelerate a child's spelling progress considerably. Helen was 11 years of age and could read very well indeed, but her spelling was atrocious. She was taught spelling by her teacher on the basis that 'being good at reading will make a good speller'. This seems to be true in some cases, but in her and her sister's cases it did not work. It took a year with another teacher who formalised spelling, and transformed Helen from a bad speller to a very good speller indeed.

ISOLATING CONCEPTS

It is vitally important to make an item clear for learning. The mind is used to selecting what it concentrates on, removing what is called background 'noise' (irrelevant material) so that a skill can be concentrated on (like driving a car) or new learning achieved.

Your child will need to **concentrate** on a spelling pattern for a short time to the exclusion of all other patterns in the environment so that **fast** and **effective** learning occurs. This, then, accounts for the difficulty many have of learning spelling through reading.

When reading, quite rightly, a child is concentrating on the **idea** in the writing, expressed by many words and sentences, and difficult spellings are therefore often overlooked. Sometimes, when a child is a very enthusiastic reader and spends a great deal of time reading, seeing particular words over and over again can result in learning spelling; but, even then, the learning links words far better in memory. John learnt to read as a baby and by three years was reading Enid

Blyton books by the score. His spelling was good, but improved rapidly in just a few weeks with spell 'grouping' so that by the age of three and a half his spelling age was twelve.

CONFUSED SCENARIO

Something else that considerably hinders learning is to present what is to be learnt closely surrounded by so-called interest material. This can divert attention, especially if the interest material is animated. Many educational adventure games (edutational) try to intermix learning and the games format, and fail because they do not make the spelling the centrepiece of what is being presented.

The trick is to provide learning in a step-wise manner and to carefully 'build' the entertainment material about it. It is important to interest your child in spelling without confusing them with a cluttered scenario. For a child this can quickly become an exercise in advanced problem-solving rather than a simple spelling exercise.

STEP-WISE LEARNING

For all children, whether fast or slow learners, it is important to build in short, easy steps onward from what they already know. If, for example, they learn the phonic letters of the alphabet, it is a relatively short step to building phonic words, b – i – n. The reason that learning fails is because the writer of a workbook, the producer of a CD Rom or a teacher has not thought through a series of linked steps in terms of what a child knows. It is important, therefore, when you select computer learning material or workbooks, that you ensure your child will learn in sensible graded steps. Bad material can only lead to discouragement and failure.

INTEREST AND CONCENTRATION

For any learner, high interest in the subject to hand means high concentration, and concentration is effectively the force that drives knowledge into memory. It is therefore important that you attempt to foster your child's interest in spelling.

This needs to be done effectively, though, so that there is active encouragement to learn. In the first place, success breeds success – the most important result of interest must be success. To encourage your child and build up their interest, only for them to fail, is counterproductive. If you are sure that workbook material or CD Rom or interest material is well presented and well structured, then your efforts to encourage will gain great benefits for your child's confidence and learning progress in spelling.

Your interest alone in their progress is motivation in itself. When you ask 'can you spell cat?', for example, and your child comes back with 'c – a – t', the sparkle in their eyes will demonstrate that there is considerable interest in there. It is important, though, not to extend the testing too far or to push too hard for answers; and you should show pleasure in even the smallest effort that they make. The 'Well done!' cannot be overdone.

There are other incentives that can be tried. In a small test, there can be the promise of an ice-cream, or some other short-term reward at the finish. Some children of this age group are also susceptible to long-term rewards – 'If you learn these few spellings we can go to the zoo next week.' A parent's role in learning is to be a motivator, and that comes from trying to be, as far as possible, the perfect parent-and-teacher. It is a subtle exercise, making learning both effective and enjoyable.

2 Phonic Spelling

This is the 'easy' type of spelling. However, you will need to check that your child's knowledge of the **short** vowels and other sounds of the phonic alphabet are well known:

a is for apple

b is for ball

c is for cup

d is for dog

e is for egg

f is for fox

g is for gate

h is for hat

i is for insect

j is for jacket

k is for kite

l is for ladder

m is for man

n is for nut

o is for orange

p is for pig

q is for queen

r is for rabbit

s is for sun

t is for tap

u is for umbrella

v is for van

w is for watch

x as in bo<u>x</u>

y is for yacht

z is for zebra

Any difficulties in forming simple three-letter words usually arise because the phonic alphabet is not learnt well enough.

FORMING THREE-LETTER PHONIC WORDS
These should represent real-life objects that your child is frequently in contact with:

'a' words   man, cat, bat, hat, dad, bag, jam, tap

'e' words   ten, pen, bed, leg

'i' words   pin, tin, pig, lip

'o' words   cot, dot, dog

'u' words   sun, mug, mum, cup, pup

These are best cut out from medium-thick card and the letters written large enough so that they can be pushed together to make a word:

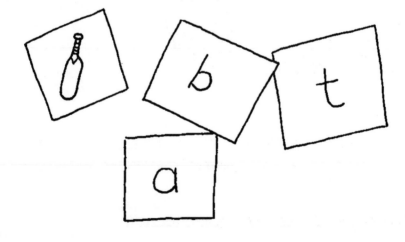

re-arranged is:

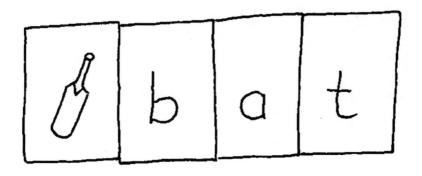

YOU CAN TRY THESE WITH YOUR CHILD

Get your child to spell out the letters of the word.

m	a	n
c	a	t
b	a	g
t	a	p
t	e	n

b	e	d
p	i	n
p	i	g
d	o	g
s	u	n
c	u	p

Some action words can be included:

r	u	n
s	i	t
h	o	p

TESTING FOR PHONIC LETTERS AND SOUNDS

The **starting letters** to words can be tested through the 'I spy' game:

'I spy with my little eye, something beginning with ...' Say any vowel beginnings as short vowels ('a' for apple, etc.).

This needs to be kept simple at first. The object (or colours) to be spotted need to be in full view, and the spoken words well known to your child.

Spotting colours ('I spy with my little eye, a colour beginning with ...') is an exercise that combines practice in recognising colours with practice on consonant sounds. The colours you test on, though, must be learnt well beforehand, otherwise the game is pointless (and very difficult for your child).

3 Learning Double Blends

Double blends are those letters at the beginnings of words that combine to make a single sound, e.g. **bl** in **bl**ot. If these are learnt as a separate exercise, spelling ability is greatly enhanced because there are many simple words that begin in this way. Some very common middles have double letters, e.g. **oo** in b**oo**t or **ee** in f**ee**t, as well as endings, e.g. e**gg**.

DOUBLE BLEND BEGINNINGS

bl	**bl**ot, **bl**ob
br	**br**ag, **br**at
cl	**cl**ap, **cl**am, **cl**ip, **cl**ub
cr	**cr**ab
ch	**ch**ip, **ch**op
dr	**dr**ip, **dr**op
fl	**fl**at
fr	**fr**og
gl	**gl**ut
gr	**gr**ub, **gr**ab

pl	**pl**ot, **pl**an
pr	**pr**am
sc	**sc**an, **sc**ab
sh	**sh**op, **sh**ip, **sh**ed
sl	**sl**ip, **sl**ap
sp	**sp**ot, **sp**in
sk	**sk**id
sw	**sw**im
th	**th**in
tr	**tr**ip, **tr**ap, **tr**ot

Using the above words with their short vowels links well with the phonics work already completed. Middles and endings that link well with this are:

oo	m**oo**n, sh**oo**t, b**oo**t, r**oo**t
ee	f**ee**t, d**ee**p, w**ee**p
gg	e**gg**
ss	le**ss**, me**ss**, to**ss**, bo**ss**
nn	i**nn**
ll	hi**ll**, pi**ll**

TRYING YOUR CHILD WITH DOUBLE BLENDS

As with the phonic work in Chapter 2, cut out cards with the main blends on one card and the vowels and consonants for several words. A picture is needed to fit with each word:

bl	o	t
cl	a	p
cr	a	b
ch	i	p
ch	o	p
dr	o	p
fr	o	g
pr	a	m

sh	o	p
sh	i	p
sp	o	t
m	oo	n
b	oo	t
f	ee	t
e	gg	
h	i	ll

It is best to teach these carefully, one at a time. Later, you can assemble a small pile representing two words with pictures, then three. It helps if you treat this sort of work as 'game playing'.

SOME DOUBLE BLEND ENDINGS

'Tick, tock goes the clock' illustrates the common use of one word ending. Such endings that link easily with previous phonic work are:

–ck clo**ck**, so**ck**, sa**ck**, ba**ck**, Ja**ck**, si**ck**

–ll i**ll**, fi**ll**, bi**ll**, Ji**ll**, she**ll**

–ing s**ing**, k**ing**, r**ing**, w**ing**

–sh fi**sh**, di**sh**, da**sh**, ca**sh**

–ch ri**ch**, mu**ch**, su**ch**

TRY YOUR CHILD WITH THESE

cl	o	ck	
s	o	ck	
sh	e	ll	
k	ing		

r	ing	

f	i	sh	

TRY THESE

Fill in the missing letter:

1 | | an |

2 | | at |

3 | | in |

4 | | ig |

5 | | un |

6 | bu | |

7 | te | |

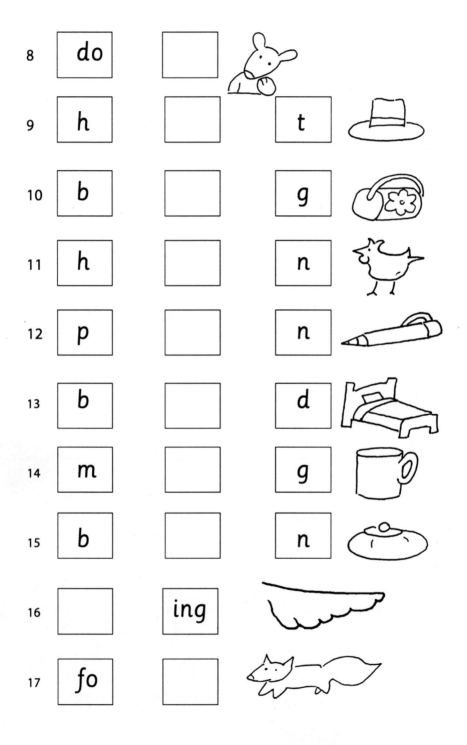

8   do   [ ]

9   h   [ ]   t

10   b   [ ]   g

11   h   [ ]   n

12   p   [ ]   n

13   b   [ ]   d

14   m   [ ]   g

15   b   [ ]   n

16   [ ]   ing

17   fo   [ ]

18 [   ] [ing]

19 [clo] [   ]

20 [fi] [   ]

21 [   ] [ag]

22 [   ] [og]

23 [   ] [um]

24 [tr] [   ] [n]

25 [   ] [ab]

26 [f] [   ] [t]

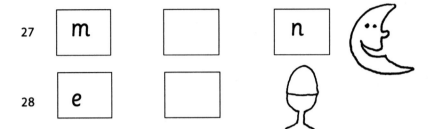

4 Magic 'e' and More Beginnings

Up to now your child has been using short vowels in phonic work – 'a' in sad, 'e' in bed, etc. Many of these words can have these short vowels changed to long vowels by the simple addition of an 'e' to the end of a word – **fad** becomes **fade**, **mad** becomes **made**, **tap** becomes **tape**. These are important words, but unfortunately, many of them represent abstract concepts (e.g. 'fade' is a difficult word for an early learner to understand). In addition to 'changing' short vowels to long vowels in words, many 'e' words have no linked phonic word, yet must have the 'e' at the end to capture the long vowel sound:

lake, page, gate, tale, mice, pole

ADDING A MAGIC 'E' TO CHANGE THE OBJECT NAME

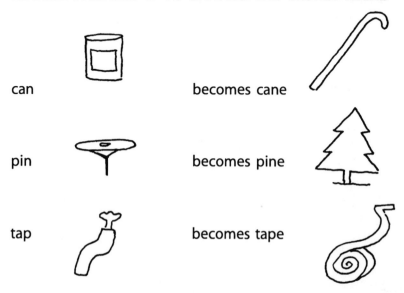

can   becomes cane

pin   becomes pine

tap   becomes tape

pan   becomes pane

hat   becomes hate

fin   becomes fine

stag   becomes stage

Other words which add 'e' but cannot always be represented by clear pictures that your child will easily understand are:

mat	to	mate
mad	to	made
rag	to	rage
wag	to	wage
sam	to	same
cap	to	cape

nap	to	nape
din	to	dine
win	to	wine
bit	to	bite
kit	to	kite
sit	to	site
hid	to	hide
not	to	note
cod	to	code
cop	to	cope
hop	to	hope
trip	to	tripe
slid	to	slide
grip	to	gripe

Help your child to get used to the difference in sound of the central vowel. Making them notice it inevitably helps memorisation.

SOME MORE BEGINNINGS

Words beginning with certain double letters can be very confusing for early learners. These letters include **qu**, **kn**, **ph** and **wh**. It helps if the words beginning with these letters represent real-life objects.

qu   for   **qu**een

kn   for   **kn**ee

kn   for   **kn**ot

kn   for   **kn**it

kn   for   **kn**ife

It needs to be explained carefully that, in these case, the **k** is a **silent** letter.

| **ph** | for | **ph**oto |
| **ph** | for | **ph**one |

And don't forget:

wh	is for	**wh**o?
wh	is for	**wh**at?
wh	is for	**wh**ere?
wh	is for	**wh**en?
wh	is for	**wh**y?
wh	is for	**wh**ich?

These are important in books and in English work in general. It is best to help your child to learn them separately. They can be written on card and used to make up a verbal sentence.

| who | what | where |

| when | why | which |

Lay these on the table and ask your child to pick the correct word card (at the beginning have a choice only between two or three). Here are some suggested sentences to say:

Who are you?

What is this? (pointing to an inanimate object)

Where is your jumper?

When is it tea-time?

Why are you so happy?

Which biscuit do you want?

Using questions like this heightens interest and focuses attention without too much stress being attached to the situation.

5 Middles and Endings

MIDDLES

Middles include double letters which are found in many words; for example, **oa** is said as a **long** 'o', as in p**o**st. They are best learnt through writing practice, through games and through association with pictures of real-life objects (where appropriate). The three parts of each word can be written large on card and fitted together with a picture:

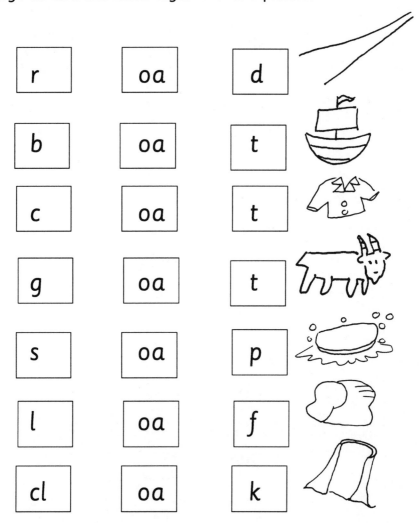

r	oa	d
b	oa	t
c	oa	t
g	oa	t
s	oa	p
l	oa	f
cl	oa	k

'ea words'

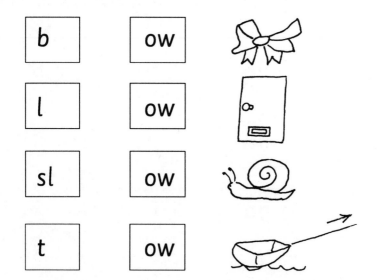

s	ea	
b	ea	d
r	ea	d
l	ea	f

'ow' and 'ou' middles

b	ow	
l	ow	
sl	ow	
t	ow	

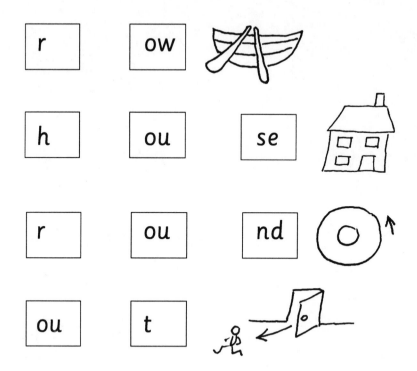

ENDINGS

These include the adding of **s** or **es** to singular words, the adding of **–ing** and some effects on preceding letters, and words ending in **–ight**.

s is the common form of plural for concrete words, and when **'es'** is added instead it is **sounded out**, e.g. wish, wishes or witch, witches. That is, with 'es' as a plural ending there is some sounding out of the 'e' part.

s- endings

toy

toys

bell

bells

apple

apples

hat

hats

cup

cups

chair

chairs

pen

pens

cat   cats

'es' plurals

fish   fishes

cross   crosses

witch   witches

wish   wishes

dish   dishes

These plurals will be easy for your child to latch on to. There are others (now in my 7–11 book) which have more difficult patterns. Three should be mentioned here because they occur very often in text for this age group:

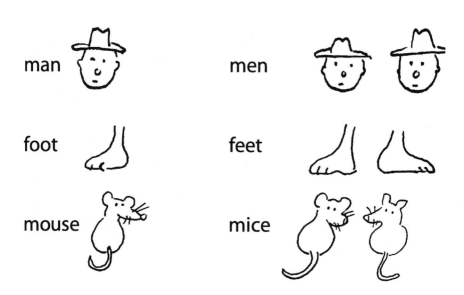

man   men

foot   feet

mouse   mice

–ing words

There are three types of additions of 'ing' to the ends of words:

1.   A straight addition of –ing:

read   read   ing

sing   sing   ing

meet   meet   ing

fish   fish   ing

play   play   ing

2.   The end letter is doubled before adding –ing.

sit   sit   ting

run   run   ning

swim   swim   ming

cut   cut   ting

tap   tap   ping

win   win   ning

3.   For words ending in 'e', the 'e' is left out when -ing is added.

like   lik   ing

bite   bit   ing

give   giv   ing

come   com ing

smile   smil ing

-ight words

Your child will be aware of most of these words through verbal communication, but the form of the words will appear strange when trying to read or spell. They are best learnt by closely relating what your child knows from real-life with the correct spelling:

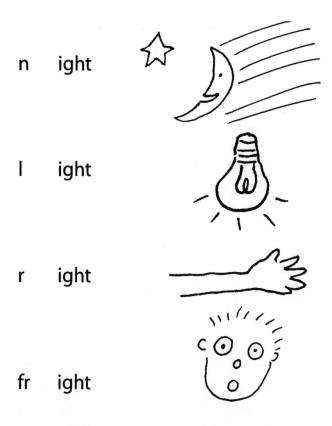

n   ight

l   ight

r   ight

fr   ight

'ay' words

There are many words with this ending, difficult to illustrate because they are often abstract, but easy to memorise because the long 'a' and 'y' can be sounded.

day, lay, say, way, hay, jay, play, pray, clay, may (or May), pay

The most useful of these words are:

d   ay

s   ay

pl   ay

pr   ay

M   ay (for the month)

TRY THESE

Add **s** or **es** to these:

toy

cup

fish

bell

day

Add **-ing** to the ends of these:

run

read

sit

bite

swim

smile

cut

sing

Get your child to put in the correct letters:

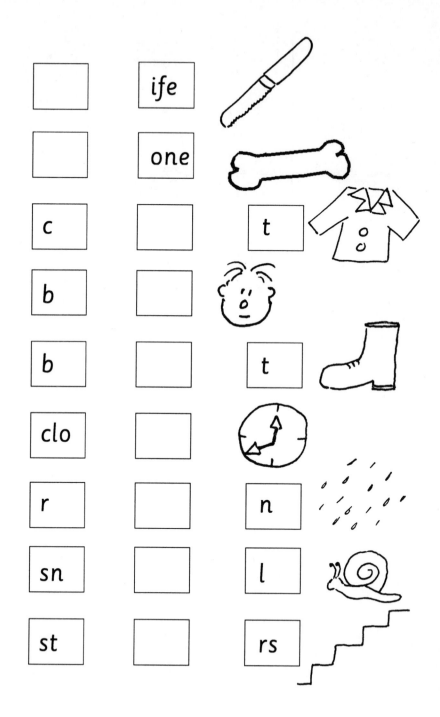

☐	ife	
☐	one	
c	☐	t
b	☐	
b	☐	t
clo	☐	
r	☐	n
sn	☐	l
st	☐	rs

6 Puzzles, Games and Crosswords to Teach Spelling

In this section there are word searches, rhyming games and crosswords for a variety of abilities.

CROSSWORDS

In these, each word is indicated by a picture at the beginning. Crosswords are in graded order.

1.

h a t

p

p i g

l

e g g

2.

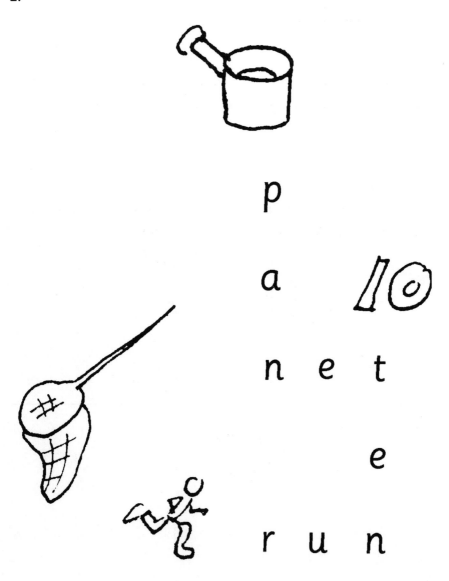

p

a

n   e   t

e

r   u   n

3.

d
o
b a g
a
t a p
n
t

4.

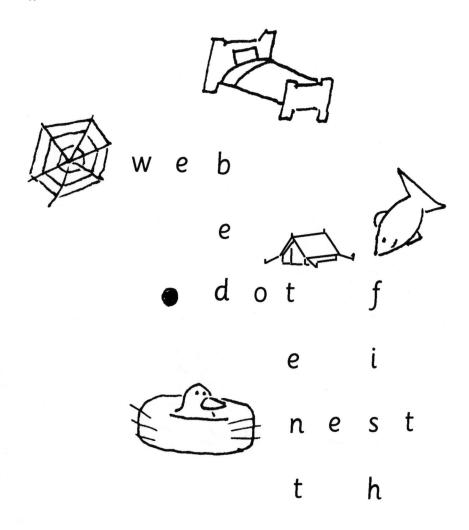

w   e   b

e

● d o t   f

e   i

n   e   s   t

t   h

5.

s u n

o

c o t

s a c k   e

h   l   n

o   o

p   c h i p

k

6.

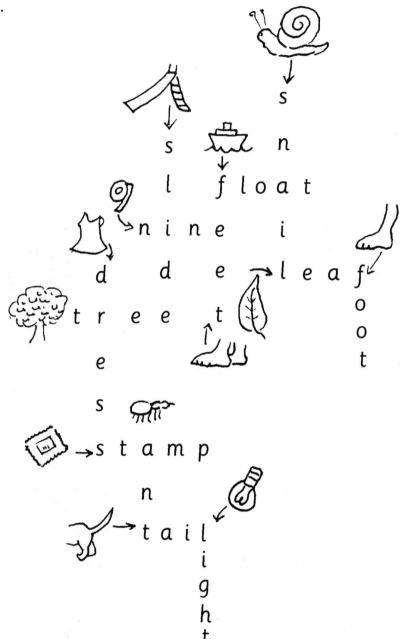

WORD SEARCHES

These are graded, from including three-letter words to those having more complex middles and endings. Words read horizontally, left to right, and vertically, downwards only.

1.

cat	a	c	a	t
pin	l	o	b	p
pig	i	t	x	i
cot	p	w	o	n
lip	z	p	i	g

cat a c a t
pin l o b p
pig i t x i
cot p w o n
lip z p i g

2.

sun p t e n t d
bat b a n t e f
tent a b g s u n
bed t a b o j k
van i g e v a n
bag n m d m n y
ant

3.

hat	f	n	p	h	a	t
flag	i	f	l	a	g	t
plum	o	g	u	n	e	f
hand	e	i	m	u	p	l
apple	d	p	h	a	n	d
nest	e	n	n	e	s	t
	a	p	p	l	e	l

4.

nest

hill

sock

king

clock

shoe

frog

grass

sheep

knife

who

t	n	e	s	t	s	t	s
f	p	e	h	i	l	l	h
r	h	s	s	h	t	k	s
o	o	o	w	c	k	n	h
g	t	c	h	h	i	i	o
o	o	k	o	k	n	f	e
c	l	o	c	k	g	e	f
s	c	i	g	r	a	s	s
s	h	e	e	p	a	g	c

RHYMING GAMES

These help with the learning of endings. Ask your child to link by pencil line the word given with the correct rhyming word:

Game 1

hat	rag
cap	run
bag	ten
mug	box
hen	mat
tin	tap
sun	rug
fox	pin

Game 2

sock	ride
hill	tail
king	boy
fish	black
lamp	coat
slide	light
snail	stamp
toy	pill
boat	wish
night	clock
sack	ring